Lisa Gorton | Hotel Hyperion

New Poems

GIRAMONDO POETS

Lisa Gorton

Hotel Hyperion

First published 2013
from the Writing & Society Research Centre
at the University of Western Sydney
by the Giramondo Publishing Company
PO Box 752 Artarmon NSW 1570 Australia
www.giramondopublishing.com

Designed by Harry Williamson
Typeset by Andrew Davies
in 10/16.5 pt Baskerville

Printed and bound by Ligare
Distributed in Australia by NewSouth Books

National Library of Australia
Cataloguing-in-Publication data:

Gorton, Lisa.
Hotel Hyperion.
ISBN 9781922146274 (pbk).
A821.3

for Kelso, Toby and Penelope

Other books by Lisa Gorton

Press Release
Cloudland

By looking into a box through a little hole one might see great plains and an immense expanse of sea spread out till the eye lost itself in the distance. Learned and unlearned agreed that these images were not like natural things but like nature itself. These demonstrations, as he called them, took place by night and day. In the former, you saw Orion, Arcturus, the Pleiades, and other shining stars, and the moon rising above high mountains; by day you saw the blaze of dawn as Homer describes it. Certain Greeks, famous men and skilled seafarers, were astonished when he showed them, in his little world, a ship far out to sea. 'Now it labours in the tempest,' he said, 'But tomorrow you will find it in the harbour.'

ANON, MID-FIFTEENTH CENTURY, *Vita anonima*

Contents

Dreams and Artefacts

Of any thing the image tell me, that
Hath kept with thy remembrance

after the Titanic Artefact Exhibition

I

Patiently, ticket by ticket, a soft-stepped crowd
advances into the mimic ship's hull half-
sailed out of the foyer wall, as if advancing into
somebody else's dream –
the interior, windowless, where perspex cases bear,
each to its single light, small relics –
a tortoiseshell comb, an ivory hand mirror,
a necklace pricked with pin's head costume pearls.
They might be mine – at least, things loosed
from a dream I had, off and on, for years.
They have suffered nothing, these things raised
from a place less like place than like memory itself –

II

Where the sea is
worked back upon itself in soundless storm,
            a staircase climbs.
Its scroll of iron foliage grows in subtler garlands now –
it is the sea's small
machinery of hunger, feeding on iron, makes these
            crookedly intricate festoons
as if it were the future of remorse overtaking – piece
by piece the staircase returns
            to the conditions of dream.

III

In the next room, they have custom-built a staircase.
A replica, reinvented from a photograph,
it leads nowhere – or it leads to the house of images
where nothing is lost. A clock without a mechanism
adorns its first floor landing, hands stopped at that minute
history pours through. We forgive things
only because we own them – This is a staircase
not for climbing, its first step strung with a soft-weave rope.

IV

It is raining as I leave –
long rain breaking itself onto the footpath,
breaking easily into the surface of itself
like a dream without emblems, an in-drawn shine.
Overhead, clouds build and ruin imaginary cities,
slow-mo historical epics with the sound down,
                    playing to no one.

The Storm Glass

If you can command these elements to silence
and work the peace of the present

A Description of the Storm Glass and Brief Guide to its Use in Forecasting Weather

I

An invention of alchemists, the first Storm Glasses were sold
under the sign of the Looking Glass on old London Bridge.
A solution of camphor sealed in glass, they mass,
weather by weather, crystalline forms that vary
with electric change in air, and make a trophy of their ruin –
so the clear spirit, which held all yesterday grey-shadowed light,
this morning raises its more precise hallucination –
these uncoloured crystals in shape resembling a Jamesian
treasury of scruples, or that more formal vaulting of remorse –

II

A sealed dome of glass where crystals,
by an alchemy 'more precise than precision', unmake
and make still grottoes that recede
from its blue-doubled curves as if epitomes
of fantastical ambition –

A replica, it would embarrass
by the overconfidence of intention, except those crystals
in colours of obduracy, which is to say,
uncoloured, blank of eye, formalise the inwardness
of weather and contract hemispheres of wind

to a decorative instance. A northerly
forms in it 'leaves of fern or yew' and, by that version of tact
which gives volume to silence,
its crystals retreat from tempest into the vanishing point
of their dimension –

III

In a Storm Glass crystals
with the exactness peculiar to foreboding make neural
flare shapes: ultrasound-
coloured threads cross-stitched with blank, as of sensation
excised and here, preserved in light.

It is tomorrow's weather
haunting a small room. Clouds, which hurry for no one,
which, amassing,
betoken that undifferentiated grudge some call ambition,
here confide motive without gesture

as if to say There is another world.
It is in this one, this sealed glass, structure of feeling
in place of thought,
where images fold into images the way a child disappears
into the film in which she plays herself –

IV

Original of Snow Domes –
soundproof rooms of repeating weather, of figurines
in time-lapse flurries
of glitter rain – not for shaking, shaken, a Storm Glass
begins again its self-assembling –

workmanship of an almost
substanceless precision. It is reinventing weather as a keepsake.
Only its double-curved glass,
which builds in parallax, makes it more like
an instrument of hauntings,
as if to say He gave his whole life to become

his idea of himself. So, tireless,
and without the extravagance of waves,
a Storm Glass amasses
its precarious adornment, this needlework in quartz,
mistakeable for regret –

V

The ambition of a miniaturist,
which fashions Mantegna's *Triumphs* in pin-scale diorama –
trophies and armour, where
Caesar's chariot by key-wound mechanism succeeds itself
upon the scene – is framed in this

where crystals, by the wreckage
upon wreckage which is making, remake weather
as a succession of rooms,
and by such recessive logic prove what is unassailable
in curios, useless things.

It is a votive of patience,
not as ships in bottles – rigged tricks of possibility –
but that experience be forfeit
to this illuminated scene, making and unmaking its alike
uninhabitable palaces –

VI

A Storm Glass belongs to winter rooms,
to where a reader, like the picture of a reader,
comes to the last page and looks up –

It is a book of hauntings.
Now on the wall by the window light
collects itself even in these rain-shadows advancing
as if concession by concession
down the rinsed shadow of the glass –
Even in these, light flares shadowless, out of scale,
the way memory makes rooms of itself
in which the simplest fact is stranger than dreams.
An heirloom carriage clock of ormolu, stopped
in its dome of glass – by such blank emblems
the house returns and it is afternoon always.
Someone is just stepping in with a tray of drinks.
The child in the window sits under their grown-up voices.
Outside a train tracks through the suburb
its vanishing point. On her lap, the Book of Reproductions
falls open at Mantegna –
that page where a soldier raising carcass-armour missteps,
stayed in a sudden doubt, and by that faltering
casts the pageant out of history, where only Caesar is –
And now the window catches light –

one of those late winter days when, an hour before sunset,
suddenly low-angled rays exaggerate the flame
and shadow of things.
Someone starts pulling the blinds.
With the first shade the house folds itself back
into the stillness of the clock –
as in a Storm Glass crystals convert the storm
to animation stills – as of the one lance
passed from hand to hand – and it is the heraldry of weather,
of clouds, all waste, and all potential –

Now the reader is walking out into the garden,
into the long rain breaking itself against the glass,
and what was soft tumult
                    proves itself new and utterly precise.

The Hotel Hyperion

Tis far off,
And rather like a dream than an assurance

I Press Release

To honour the Year of Perfected Vision, in 2020 the PDK-4 Corporation signed up its first Hibernation Astronaut for the missile 'After life', launching its Perpetual World Campaign: 'Preserving Our Most Beautiful Offspring for the New Life on Titan...'

They chose my child. I visit him
daily in the tiled room. His naked skin
looks backed with ice. I see his heart
beat hourly on the screen. He is safe,
I know, for his will be an innocent world,
conquered in peace.
                He does not breathe
more than once a heartbeat. My own
small breaths haunt the cold when I speak
into the audiofile they have contracted to play
across his light years on repeat. 'Don't be afraid,'
I say. 'Like a handshake, palm to palm,
                a gentleman's agreement,
your heartbeat tenders you – Are you cold?
Listen, out of these bypassed years,
silence in your mouth, you will amass such –
Only to think of you, falling from your name for sky
in this astonishing vessel!
                Press release, my darling,
and do not sorrow. Do not once sorrow.
If you will think of me, think only of these years
I held your unfailing present in my empty hands.'

II The History Of Space Travel

In truth, the history of space travel
is a history of rooms
            – I kept a room
those eleven years in the Hotel Hyperion.
It had been a prison, the first in orbit,
and its guest rooms kept the old locks.
The Futures Museum was paying me for artefacts
from the failed outposts of settlement
            – Those years, voyaging
to the forsaken places, I slept
more than I woke, never shaking off
the after-weight of anaesthetic sleep
before I slept again – places that held then
in my mind like so many self-lit dreams
but for the relics I brought back
            – I used to time my waking
for the radio line where their abandoned
voices first shaped words in static
the way a figure wades out of mirage
dripping with light – Whispers, pleas,
accusations, prayers – voices in their afterlife
talking me out of sleep.

III Screen, Memory

When I try to remember those years,
I see the room
                    – the Hotel was a prototype
too expensive to copy, a mined-out moon
inside so self-consistent
its corridors turned into themselves.
I was forever stepping from a mirror
                    – In place of windows, the room had screens
playing images of where we were. We might have been
travelling into the space inside a TV. Images,
fed from outboard cameras on delay. Like any trick of memory
they closed a wilderness in glass
                    – technicolour galaxies
fitted to the room, cameras that made each thing
speak itself in light. They had no vanishing point.
Only detail by detail they installed themselves in me,
screens I watched until their distances were mine
                    – It is like trying to enter again
some old obsession. Once I walked a bush track
where new rain made its slow mimicry of wind's sound –
one craving built of exact and various falls.
But I was never there. It must have been a film I watched
and have it still
                    – my own, and not my own.

IV Settlement, Titan

Fanatics have their dreams, wherewith they weave
a Paradise for a sect… Keats, 'The Fall of Hyperion'

This glassed-in world the scale of memory, self-
        possessing its own loss.
Here, never the small, slant rain that is intimate
        because it does not know you –
Only this path beneath a trellis weighed with vines
        by fruit trees under lights,
the bright fruit set in many-shadowed leaves –

Rooms within a room: a structure of vaults
        that holds in air,
its whirr of engines subdued to the sound of bees
        eating out palaces
in fallen fruit – Seasons built into the lights, and here
        the bright fish turn
as if by clockwork in the clear-walled stream –

It is so orderly and strange. A sort of camera obscura
        that would teach how to make
the illusion of depth on paper, which is to say
        they lived their whole lives here –
I am collecting things as they were in somebody else's dream,
        trading in years for them
as though the dream were mine.

V Discovery

Routine search, Kuiper Peninsula.
This blank of Titan where the wind is
visible, anodised with cold –
                    I don't hear it.
I am closed in my life, my machine-
fed breath, a true ghost haunting
the loneliest idea –
                    walking out
from the settlement's small world
of manufactured atmosphere. Strange to see
and not to feel the cold –
                    this ice-waste eating
rifts into itself, fitted to the screen
as if to say 'I have walked through mirrors,
shrinking to scale
                    self-lit worlds' –
Then to come on the wreck, its landing chute
ice-caught, flaring, torn throat of the wind's cry up-
flung tirelessly
                    out of itself –
and like pure fiction the ship, propped in debris –
years lost to a trick of light – the door sealed in ice
it will take days to clear –
                    That instant I see them
in my mind as they will be found, unwaking,
stored in the machinery of patience,

in their Perspex coffers
blindly face to face and nothing decayed –
Only, on their ice-backed skin
this filigree of ice
the machine is breathing them, resembling
the mechanism of a clock copied in snow.

The Futures Museum: The Sleepers

resin, oils, human hair, camphor solution (potassium nitrate, ammonium chloride, water, ethanol, camphor), fishing wire

In this display the artist
has wrapped life-cast figures in a hand-
made net of fishing wire – Figures
painted with a one-hair brush and true
even to the number of their eyelashes, the blind
sheen of their nails – so much like life
they bring home the strangeness of things
being motionless.

Only the net,
its each thread soaked in camphor solution,
grows counterfeit ice, first as if by fraying,
by threads so fine as to be speculative –
each thread the colour of a needle-scratch
in glass – and they divide from each division
till like regret, which feeds on hunger, they
close in the effigies –

as if they would prove
by what trick of longing the blankest fact is
closed in dreams the way a new-hatched bird's
bluish flesh-clot pricks with feathers, each exact
as fossil etchings, and it is the blood-fist free
in its device – Some force there is will be consoled,
will make these votives of a stranger's loss.
Of any stranger's loss.

The Futures Museum: Night Guard

For Sarah Tutton

I

Rooms so familiar
they complete themselves in me –
this darkened hall where the glass cases,
pent with light, are like train windows at night
taking the light with them into that long roar –
I am waiting at the crossing gate
in rain so soft it is an easing of the dark,
surprised by so many small persisting sounds,
everywhere rain stepping leaf by grass blade down
into its earth –
as if to say imagery
is not invented. Even the simplest fact is
at each instant folding itself in light, is
opening out into false perspectives the way
in each glass pane the doubling reflection
of a thing stands farther off and smaller,
farther off and so far gone into a trick of longing
now the night cleaners, bound to their machines,
with bowed heads pass modestly
among hallucinated corridors –

II

In the next room screens,
which all day dream a ship engulfed in light,
in the white burn of its engines, shouldering
massively free – and dream a ship
engulfed in light, as if to prove the meaning
of repetition – overnight close in
the railway embankment where I walked as a child
into the holding place –
ground so dedicated to its purpose
it stopped existing between trains,
where the aniseed flourished soft plumes
in colours drawn out of shadow, out of
the sparsest shadow finely, and where
the long tracks, sheering off, held a sky-gleam
chancily, like tension in a green stick plied
between two hands –
into the dispossessed place –
along the side of the house, in the dusty undermess
of a jasmine arch, wherever sour ground was
netted with dank weeds – where I called things mine
because they haunted me.

III

And because out-of-date technology
endears lost futures to us, among the screens they keep
a miniature Diorama – a foot-square box that holds
Titan's abandoned settlement,
its vaulted dome and gardens, built to scale, intricate
with fruit trees and mechanic streams which here
unfold
less like natural things than like nature itself –
and nowhere waste,
as if we had conquered here that feat of memory
which makes a whole world wait upon a small room,
where the figures, now they have stopped their clock-
work motion, stand amazed in a fall of light
like things newborn –
That figure with her back turned,
disappearing from the scene, is the Collector,
bearing off the relic found in her possession when she
died –
one of those glass domes with a backdrop sky, a sea
of dissatisfied small waves – its plastic ship full-rigged
and canting in the glitter storm.

Room and Bell

Yea all which it inherit, shall dissolve

At which point unexpectedly, sorting through a box of toys, I found that brass bell which stood beside my bed through all that childhood illness, and which, though I had long since forgotten it, kept still the power of summoning people to my room…

I

I rang the bell and they came. The bell was made of brass cast in the figure of a woman dressed in crinoline. Her body fitted the crease of my palm. Straight-backed, arms akimbo, with her hair in a topknot, her breasts like elbows, she had the look of someone preparing a rebuke. Only when I lifted her from the shelf, I saw how helplessly her legs, swing-jointed at the hips, jigged against her skirts, and as I swung her from side-to-side, I knew how it would nourish in her the longing to make the world wait upon a small room. I rang the bell and they came: one of my brothers perhaps – more likely, my sister or my mother. Memory recasts them as figures so tall they had to bow their heads to step into the room. Coming to the door, they had the light behind them. They cast their long shadows across my carpet. Their annoyance did not disturb me. It proved the power of my bell, which had summoned them against their will from the midst of days.

II

Whatever time they came to the door, they had the light behind them. My room was planted in the shade of an ornamental pear tree. The tree is there still, though the room has gone. Even as I write this, its green light builds itself around me; again its glass-grey leaf-shadows advance from the wall behind my bed up to the ceiling. They turn over in the wind: a motion so closely resembling the sound of slow-running water that as I watch them I hear again the stream which ran once where now the garden is. That imaginary sound underran all my hours in that room just as, now, the memory of that room underruns alike my images of home and my desire to collect things closed in glass – For, holding a Snow Dome in my hand, watching the last glitter settle on its plastic ship and backdrop waves, I recover the experience of that hour when, folding down a corner of my book, I watched the leaf-shadows turning over on the ceiling and claimed as my own those freedoms founded on retreat.

III

A bland, small room – nothing about it accounts for the feelings that it lodged in me. Not the built-in wardrobe, the pine desk under the window, not the two shelves lined with books above my bed, not the high window which remade weather as a moving picture – I have set out the furniture as it would appear to someone standing in the doorway, looking clockwise, though in my memory, the room builds itself out from where I sit in bed, first as the presence, there, in front of me, of a rectangle of light, then as the consciousness of that light's shadow on the wall behind me. This moment, I know the room not as a place, not even as a memory, but as though some ghost of the future had whispered in my ear, 'Here you are', and permitted me to glimpse, this moment, the room as it will be when it exists only by my haunting. This trick of memory, this O, which builds itself out of fragments, out of a structure of shadows, in which I can no longer distinguish between memories and objects, in which the very door handle and skirting boards, as they assume their shapes, appear to me still in the unreal light of that first moment – it is by this that I enter into the dream that a place is mine.

IV

In truth, that dreamt-up room has less in common with my room as it was than it has with those rooms that build themselves in my mind when I am reading – rooms which, the moment I pause to examine them, turn out to be made of one or two furnishings set among struts of light – a notion of depth and width and height built out of prepositions, out of a speaker's tone of voice. Though they are sketched in light, I am conscious of them not as I would see them but as I would remember the formation of a room in the dark. My imagination has troubled to manufacture one detail fully: a blue and white teacup with a stone fleck in the porcelain an inch from its inside rim. A slightly tarnished teaspoon in the saucer shows, upside down, the reflection of a window. These rooms that build themselves in my mind when I am reading take their effect of truth – which, since they are not true, is an effect of feeling – from that first room, which, since it installed itself in me, has stood behind so many other rooms, concealed itself in so many other places, tricked me so many times into a feeling of homecoming – which has travelled so much farther than I have.

V

In this architecture, which is built in us, there is no part so unpossessed as hallways, which must be hung with etchings and reproductions, with landscapes constructed upon a vanishing point. No domestic interior can work there, no picture of a woman reading – for see how ill at ease she looks! She wants to read to the end of the chapter; she keeps glancing at her watch. Soon it will be time to collect the children; she has not yet started on the ironing or hung the washing out. Light from the doorway throws its bright blank onto the picture glass, a skewed rectangle in which my shadow floats, reduced to the scale of her room and yet stopped at the edge of it. If from time to time the woman reading has an uneasy sense that there, on the other side of the glass, stands the child that she was, watching from a doorway, this is only because that child remembers, late one afternoon, glancing up from her kitchen work to find the shadow of a woman seated on the kitchen table, watching her with that same cool pressure of attention, which makes a stranger in the street turn around, sensing our eyes on her back.

VI

That room has gone, the wall knocked out to extend the living room. Now a sofa rests against the wall where my bed was. I settle there when I visit my mother's house. Every familiar place has this more intimate architecture: these structures of memory, which build our shelter within the shelter of a house. To discover it, I need only step blindfolded through the door. At once the house builds itself around me, not as rooms and not equally, but as habits belonging to left and right, to close and farther off. The true translation of my experience of a house would be: the place where I go between; the place of being careful; the place where I hid once behind the chair (the place of skirting boards); the place built about a trapdoor that each night drops me through the floor of my own being.

The Triumph of Caesar

But how is it

That this lives in thy mind? What seest thou else …

The Humanity of Abstract Painting

for Diena Georgetti

I

Afternoon rain on the windows,
bare rooms stilled with light – an idea of the house
that had always haunted your life in it,
as if to say This is the machine of the present.
It reinvents experience as a daydream.
This is the empty house –

II

The rain sound is less like sound than it is
the trick of familiar places, which holds things
in the blank of your eye.
Boxes filled with what you own. Now
room after room you make this more entire
architecture of memory –

III

An infinite of loss closed in its frame
like the house of a modernist: furniture fit to the room.
Everything thought, every thing
remembered, as if somebody else's house
now has you in it, a collector of things as they were
in somebody else's dream –

IV

Because a collector is free
as facing mirrors prove the renewal in what it is
to be possessed. Rooms you could walk through
blind, windows of rain-coloured light.
This is the house that silence returns to you.
This is the empty house.

Soft Tissue

after Michelle Nikou

A cupboard of tissue boxes
so when you cried I had some
soft thing I could tear –
Here, press your tears into my hand.
This is what the forest was ruined for –
tissues which fold out one in one,
indifferently soft. Don't cry.
The forest was ruined for this,
the quick-growing pine's invented
vanishing points along a far ridge
cut to this, an inside-out look
to its cleared ground. Don't cry –
Back then, weekly I emptied bins
of the soft-ply, tear-sated things.

Mistletoe

for Rebecca Mayo

A subtler haunting, as mistletoe
subdues its leaf to the host, possessed
by what it feeds on – Still
its lopsided chandelier flourishes
on the stricken branch where self-
defeating pride, dignity's withdrawn
sad smile, furnish no room.
Upon necessity's crooked vaulting –
that drawn-out bewilderment
called making do – it offers up
its ripe berry, its indigestible seed.

Homesickness

In 2008, the British artist, Roger Hiorns, pumped 80,000 litres of copper sulphate solution into a condemned flat which, after two weeks, was overtaken by crystals. He called the work, 'Seizure'.

Now nothing of the lived-in place
but like a work of memory, where the flood was, insatiate
the crystals mass edge upon edge and,
self-repeating, consume scale models of themselves
like facing mirrors, haunted by the rooms they make –
rooms where you stand among the furnishings
alike simplified, alike held in a trick of light –
and they advance by repetition, axiom by axiom
they show how facts enter into the machinery of dreams,
for here are broken fittings strung in mimic globes,
windows as of crushed glass grown upon itself
a treasury of jewels not worth trade –
Like patience made into a way of life, its walls close in
the flood again in time-lapse, unwithdrawing waves.

Freeways

Cities make such small use of clouds.
Only when you turn onto freeways, the sky comes back to you
like the idea of some more spacious life –

I remember freeways
from the back seat of my parents' car.
Paddocks going out ignorant as clouds,
country that makes nothing and is permanent.
Dead trees stick up, one or two in every paddock,
bone-dry, driftwood-grey – boredom has done that,
worn them to this stripped and isolate simplicity,
propped out there not like trees that ever were
but like a whale's tooth, or a wishbone –
Here a foundered pony picks among tasselled rust-weed
in ground left over between a tractor warehouse
and a petrol station with its single bowser,
its 6 by 12 shed with the glass kicked in, where even
the graffiti is rusted. The motel is not real enough
to be haunted – You know the place, where
you need to cram in by the basin to close the bathroom door,
where the periscope-shaped hairdryer turned to the wall
has earned the motel sign a half-star extra. There it is,
over VACANCY –

The Triumph of Caesar

after Mantegna

I

The trumpeters have gone ahead.
                    Morning of high, quick clouds –
He learned to paint on broken statues.
In his pictures, the weather looks real, the people
dressed in stone – bright, wind-caught stone – and stayed
in the gesture of a statue, the iconography of feeling
waiting in the flesh like animation stills.
Slow work of years, unfinished – work made
for the passageway of a Palace, where you keep stepping back
and back to see the thing entire – He has copied,
with the brushstrokes of a miniaturist, facts that are lost:
trophies and armour from a stone frieze
where now the market is, as if he could by that precision
free these spoils of the Triumph – That soldier
bearing the empty armour high on a cross –
armour encased in dragon scales, its metal body strangely
eaten out, like apple casings at the end of summer
in the grass – that soldier missteps and looks down.
It is the gesture of remembering. The Triumph folds,
perspective by perspective, into that vanishing point –

II

The trumpeters have gone ahead.
                    The picture is mostly of legs –
it shows the Triumph from a child's viewpoint.
Soldiers and horses – so many, they crowd
perspective out. Only a few figures stand entire
at the boundary of the picture as if they would step
the next instant into that vast which is not there –
The pattern their legs make repeats
the pattern of lances, angles drawn against the clouds
like a working out of every possibility. Captured arms,
bulls crowned for sacrifice, prisoners, victories and
loads of coin, spears and catapults, colossal statues, elephants –
sights that replace each other, new and again
new, the way I remember highways from the back seat
of my parents' car – fields stacked with light
which did not pass but poured through me – Procession
so massed and intricate, here and again on their painted placards
where boys on fine-boned horses drag siege equipment
to the walled city and the city is their backdrop
and its backdrop is the sky –

III

The trumpeters have gone ahead.
                    Even from their calves,
from the balls of their feet, breath strains upwards
to the trumpet's mouth. They have closed their lips
on metal. Now they cry with its voice, bright
uncompanionable cry – It is the picture's only sound.
Catcalls, the jitter of harness, these you imagine
poised in that next instant when the horse's hoof
will fall, the chariot advance –
Only metal has changed the colour of the light,
making it colder even where it shines
alike on gold and bronze and polished lead –
Even the clouds look brittler with the light
struck off bright, blind metal –
Casually the soldiers walk after the trumpet's cry.

Notes

The epigraph to this collection comes from an anonymous fifteenth-century manuscript, cited in Samuel Y. Edgerton's *The Mirror, the Window, and the Telescope: How Renaissance Linear Perspective Changed the Vision of the Universe*. The quotes that form epigraphs to each part of the book come from *The Tempest*. The poem, 'Press Release', is reprinted from my 2007 collection of that name, because it forms the starting point for the 'Hotel Hyperion' sequence in this collection.

Acknowledgements

Some of these poems first appeared in: *Antipodes* (US), *The Australian Book Review*, *Arena*, *Age*, *Axon*, Black Inc's *Best Australian Poems* 2008, 2009, 2010, 2011, 2012, *Ekleksographia*, *The Griffith Review*, *Mantis* (US), *Melbourne University Magazine*, *Thirty Australian Poets*, and the Turnrow (US) *Series of International Literature: Australia* (forthcoming); as well as *Mistletoes of Southern Australia* and *English for the Australian Curriculum: Interactive Textbook*.

Antoni Jach generously offered advice on this collection. Sarah Tutton's commissions prompted several of these poems. Anne Brumfitt and Lachlan Thompson shared their knowledge of space technology and exploration. I am grateful to the Reading Poets and to those involved in the 2011 APC/RMIT writer-in-residence program, which afforded me time to complete several of these poems; to Val Creese, Barbara Everett and Chris Wallace-Crabbe for their teaching and encouragement; and to Sue Gorton and John Wentworth for longstanding support. Above all, I thank my editor Ivor Indyk.

Also to curators and artists who commissioned poems for catalogues: *Regeneration* (Rebecca Mayo and Marion Crawford, The Project Space, RMIT), *Before & After Science: 2010 Adelaide Festival Biennial* (eds Sarah Tutton and Charlotte Day), and *Star Voyager: Exploring Space on Screen* for Australian Centre of the Moving Image (eds Sarah Tutton and Emma McCrae). I thank Rebecca Mayo, Diena Georgetti and Michelle Nikou for discussing their work with me and allowing me to write about it. The title 'The Humanity of Abstract Painting' is taken from one of Diena Georgetti's paintings.

This project has been assisted by the Victorian Government through the Arts Victoria Developing Writers' Program and by the Commonwealth Government through the Australia Council, its arts funding and advisory body.